# WOULD AN ELEPHANT

# ENJOY THE SEASIDE?

...and other questions

Aleksei Bitskoff &
Camilla de la Bédoyère

African elephants are the largest

Design: Duck Egg Blue
Editor: Carly Madden
Editorial Director: Victoria Garrard
Art Director: Laura Roberts-Jensen
Associate Publisher: Maxime Boucknooghe
Publisher: Zeta Jones

Copyright © QED Publishing 2015

First published in the UK in 2015 by
QED Publishing
Part of The Quarto Group
The Old Brewery
6 Blundell Street
London N7 9BH

www.qed-publishing.co.uk

A catalogue record for this book is available from the British Library.

ISBN 978 1 78171 585 7

Printed in China

animals that live on land.

They live in family groups and stroll through forests and grasslands together.

Imagine if an African elephant came to stay. What would she do?

What if an elephant wanted to go upstairs?

Climbing up the stairs is not a big problem...

...but coming down again is.

Elephants are HUGE, heavy animals.

Their front legs can't take the weight of their bodies as they climb down the stairs.

An African elephant can weigh more than 5 tons!

What would an elephant like for breakfast?

She has a **BIG** appetite so she might try to eat everything that grows.

A baby elephant drinks 10 litres of milk a day – that's enough milk to fill 40 bottles.

Meanwhile, Mum could munch her way through

# 1400 apples!

# Could an elephant join an art class?

Yes, elephants are clever animals.
They can learn how to do new things.

In the wild, elephants use sticks to...

...scratch their bottoms!

So, an elephant could easily hold a paintbrush in her trunk.

# Would an elephant enjoy a trip to the seaside?

She might get burned, unless she was smothered in suncream!

Elephants have thick, wrinkly skin but it can still get sore in the sun.

In the wild, elephants roll around in mud, which protects their skin from the hot sun.

If she got hot, she could flap her ENORMOUS ears to cool down.

The moving air takes heat away from her body.

# How would an elephant say "hello"?

When they want to talk, elephants raise their trunks and trumpet...

QUIET PLEASE

...very loudly!

They also talk to each other by making low rumbling sounds that pass down their legs and into the ground.

Far away, other elephants feel the rumbles through the soles of their feet.

# What would an elephant do at playtime?

She wouldn't skip because elephants can't jump, and she is far too heavy for the swings.

She could help make a see-saw though!

An elephant can use her strong trunk to lift...

250 kilograms.

A baby elephant weighs the same as eight children!

# Could an elephant be a ballet dancer?

Her feet are bigger than **dinner plates,** so she wouldn't look very elegant!

Elephants need big feet to carry all that weight.

She would also find it hard to point her toes. African elephants have four toenails on a front foot, and three toenails on a back foot.

Could an elephant snorkel?

A trunk is a nose, so when elephants swim **underwater** they can use their trunks like a snorkel to breathe.

All elephants love to swim and play in the water. They turn their trunks into **power showers** and spray themselves clean.

An elephant's trunk is the biggest nose in the world.

What if a baby elephant needs a nap?

He could take a nap
standing up, or he might
lie down for a longer sleep.
He is too heavy for a bed!

A baby elephant would like a bedtime cuddle. Elephants hug by wrapping their trunks around each other.

Baby elephants don't have **thumbs to suck,** but their trunks do the job just as well!

# More about African elephants

Elephant is pointing to the place where she lives.
Can you see where you live?

## FACT FILE

An elephant family is ruled by a mother or grandmother. She is called the matriarch.

The longest tusks ever seen on an elephant measured more than 3 metres long.

Adult male elephants are called bulls and they usually live alone.

When an elephant is born its trunk is floppy. The baby must learn how to use it like a hand.

Elephants will go on very long walks – up to 40 kilometres a day – to find water or tasty fruit to eat.

Areas where African elephants live

NORTH AMERICA

PACIFIC OCEAN

SOU AMEF

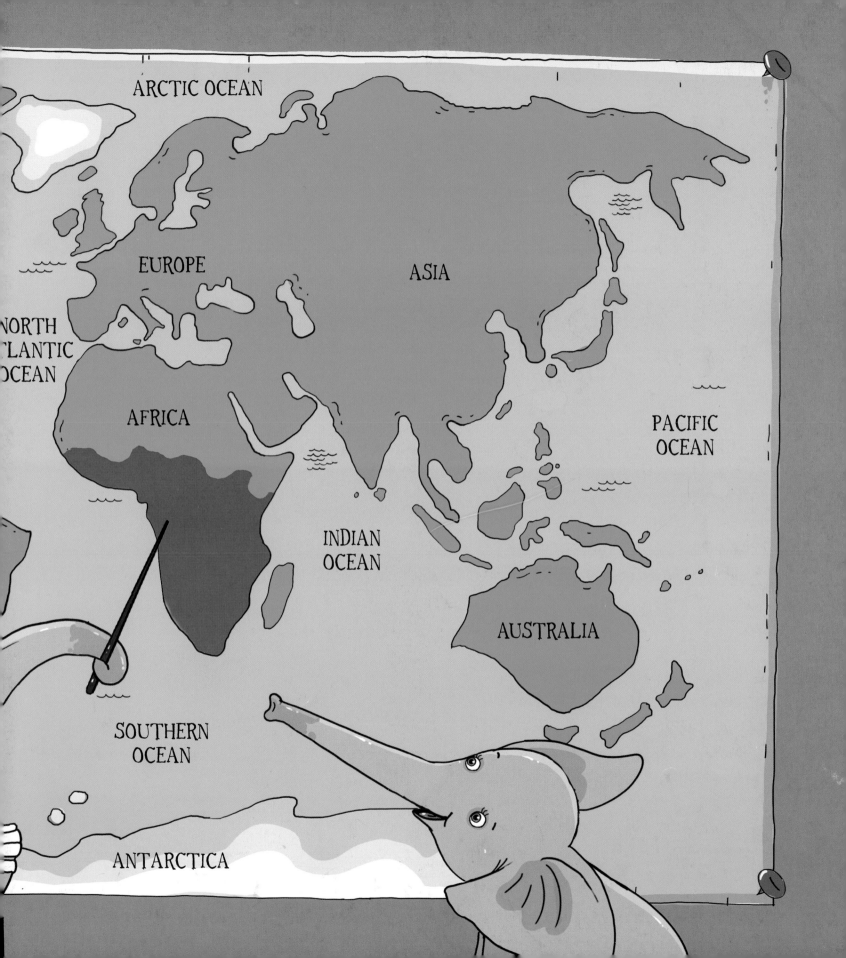

# Greetings from Africa!

# POST CARD

Thank you for looking after us so well, we had lots of fun! Grandma was very pleased with the paintings I did for her. Tomorrow we are going on a long walk through the forest because we heard there is plenty of juicy fruit that is ripe and ready to eat. Yum!

Love,
Elephant (and Baby) X x

SENT BY AFRICAN ELEPHANT POST
AFRICAN FOREST, GAMBON, AFRICA

1ST

The Johnson Family
189 Long Road
Hertfordshire
EN8 5TP
UK

5148263560809178379